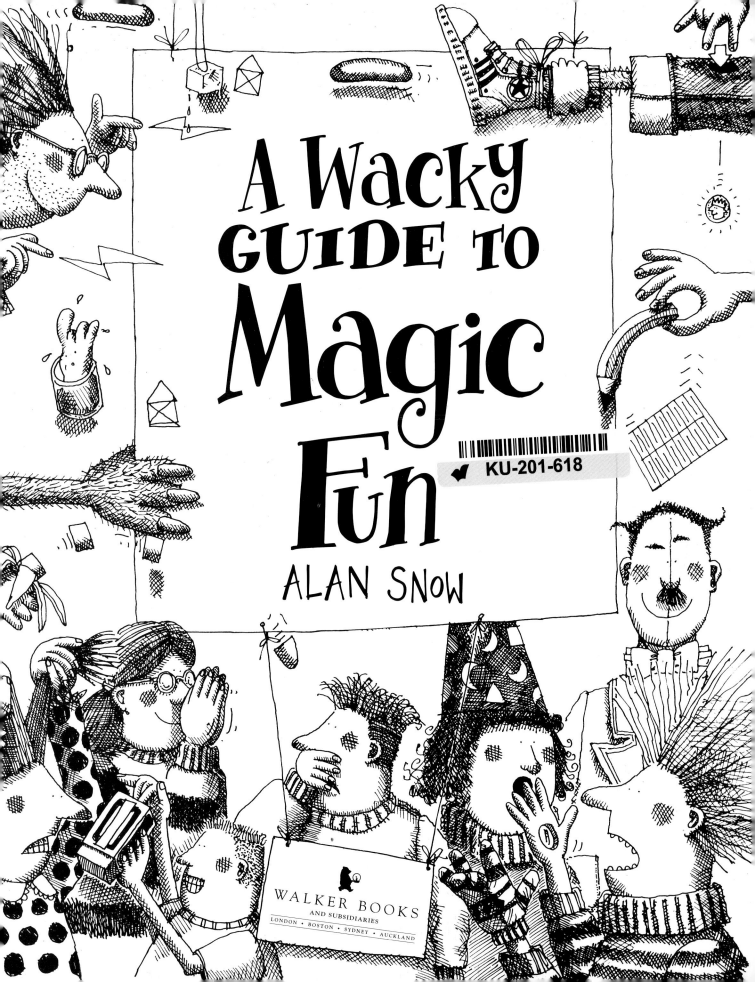

A Wacky Guide to Magic Fun

ALAN SNOW

WALKER BOOKS
AND SUBSIDIARIES
LONDON · BOSTON · SYDNEY · AUCKLAND

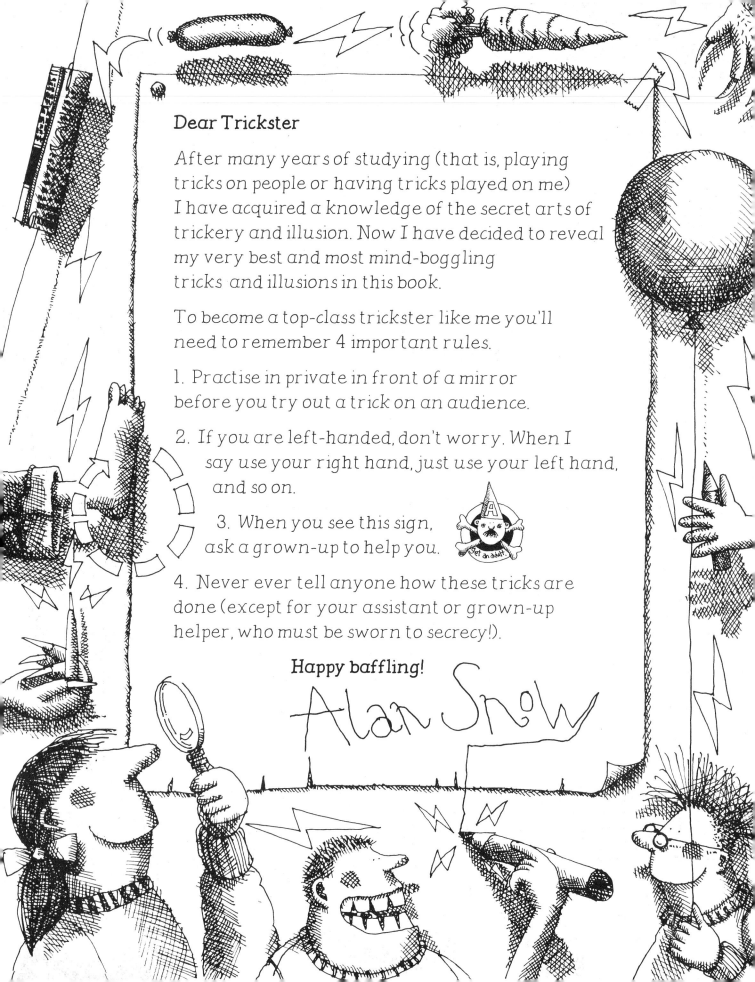

Dear Trickster

After many years of studying (that is, playing tricks on people or having tricks played on me) I have acquired a knowledge of the secret arts of trickery and illusion. Now I have decided to reveal my very best and most mind-boggling tricks and illusions in this book.

To become a top-class trickster like me you'll need to remember 4 important rules.

1. Practise in private in front of a mirror before you try out a trick on an audience.

2. If you are left-handed, don't worry. When I say use your right hand, just use your left hand, and so on.

3. When you see this sign, ask a grown-up to help you.

4. Never ever tell anyone how these tricks are done (except for your assistant or grown-up helper, who must be sworn to secrecy!).

Happy baffling!

Alan Snow

Contents

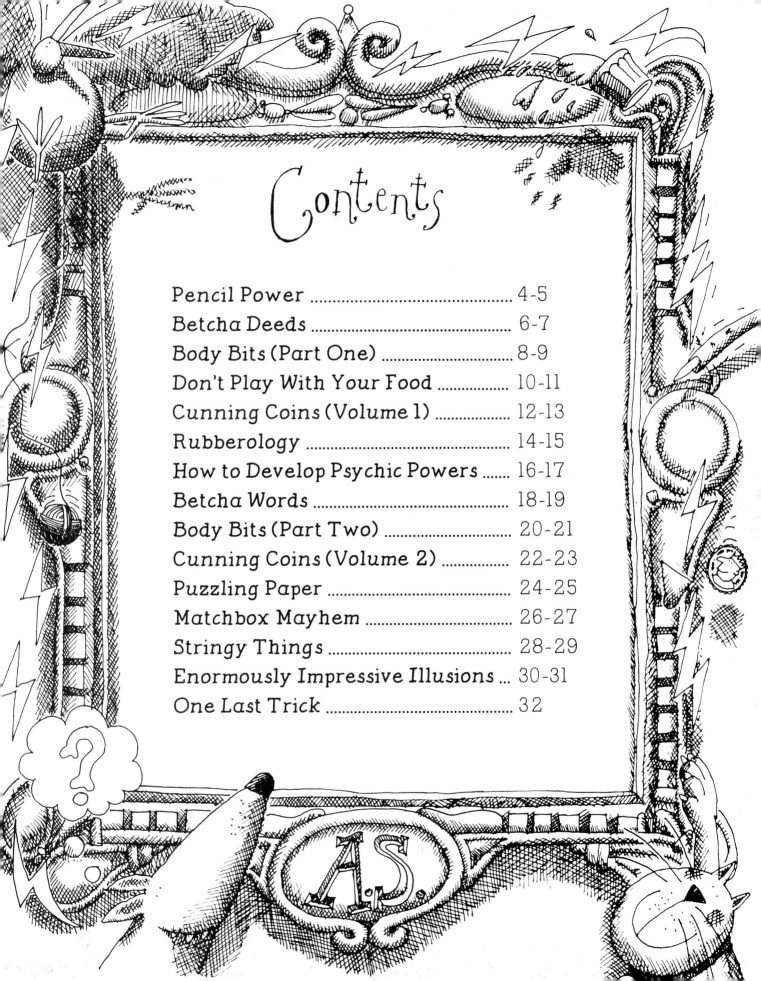

Magnetic Finger

You need a small, round pencil or a crayon.

1. Place the pencil on a smooth, flat surface.

2. Put the forefinger of one hand in front of the pencil.

3. Secretly, blow at the pencil.

4. As the pencil starts rolling away from you, slowly move your forefinger along the surface in front of it. It will look as though your finger is pulling the pencil by magnetic power.

Bendy Pencil

You need a long pencil.

Hold the pencil quite loosely at the blunt end, and waggle it from side to side. The straight pencil will look as if it's bent.

Pencil

Sticky Pencil

You need a pencil.

1. Stand sideways in front of your audience, hold out your left hand, palm up, and put the pencil across it.

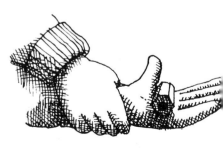

2. Grab your left wrist.

Winking Face

You need a sheet of white paper 18 cm long and 4 cm wide, some tracing-paper, a pencil, and some sticky tape.

1. Fold the strip of paper in half to make a booklet.

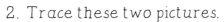

2. Trace these two pictures.

3. Put Picture 1 onto the middle of the first page of the booklet, and Picture 2 onto the middle of the second page.

4. With a piece of sticky tape, stick the pencil onto the cut end of the first page.

5. On a firm surface, roll the first page tightly round the pencil as far as the picture, holding the folded edge firmly with one hand.

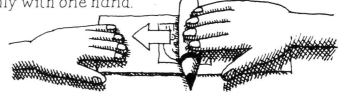

6. Now quickly move the pencil backwards and forwards across the second page to make the face wink!

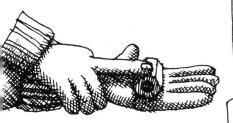

3. Turn your left hand so the audience can only see the back, secretly putting your right forefinger across the pencil to hold it.

4. The audience will think the pencil is sticking to your hand!

Magic Circle

You need a pencil and a sheet of paper.
Say, "BET YOU can't draw a circle with a dot in the middle without taking the pencil-tip off the paper."
HOW TO DO IT:

1. In one corner of the paper draw a big circle. Leave the tip of the pencil on the paper.

2. With your other hand, fold over the corner of the paper so that the folded corner comes to a point in the middle of the circle.

3. Carry on drawing round the circle and across the piece of folded paper to the point. Make a dot in the middle of the circle.

4. Now fold back the corner of the paper and take your pencil away. Hey presto! A dot in a circle!

Betcha

Bet your friends they can't do any of these difficult deeds. Then show them how, when they fail!

Hurricane Puff

You need a big, thick book and a paper bag. Stand the book upright on a table and say, "BET YOU can't blow this book over."

HOW TO DO IT:
1. Put the paper bag flat on the table, with the open end of the bag hanging over the edge of the table.

2. Stand the book on the paper bag.

3. Now scrunch up the open end of the bag to make a neck and blow into it. The book will fall over!

Deeds

Right-Hand Foot

Say, "BET YOU can't stand on your left leg, swing your right foot in a circle clockwise and, at the same time, write a 6 with your right hand."

HOW TO DO IT:
The secret is to write the 6 clockwise.

One Line House

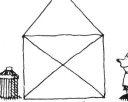

You need a pencil and a sheet of paper.

Copy the drawing of the house onto a sheet of paper. Now show your drawing to some friends and say, "BET YOU can't draw this house without going over any of the lines or taking the tip of the pencil off the paper."

HOW TO DO IT:
Look at the picture.

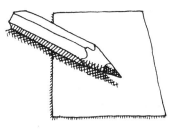

finish ■   ● start!

Peg Leg

Say, "BET YOU can't stand sideways with one leg pressed against a wall, and lift your other leg."

HOW TO DO IT:
You can't! You'll fall over!

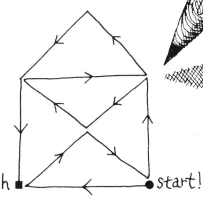

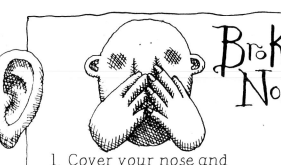

Broken Nose

1. Cover your nose and mouth with both your hands.

2. Push the end of your nose from side to side.

3. At the same time, secretly flick a thumbnail against one of your top teeth.

yuk!

It'll look and sound as if your nose is broken!

WARNING Make sure yo

Some of the

(Part

Dead Finger

Press your palm against a friend's palm. With the finger and thumb of your other hand rub gently, up and down, against the 2 pressed-together forefingers.
One finger will feel dead. Whose?

Horrible Teeth

try different teeth shapes !?!...

You need a large segment of orange peel and some scissors.

Now smile!

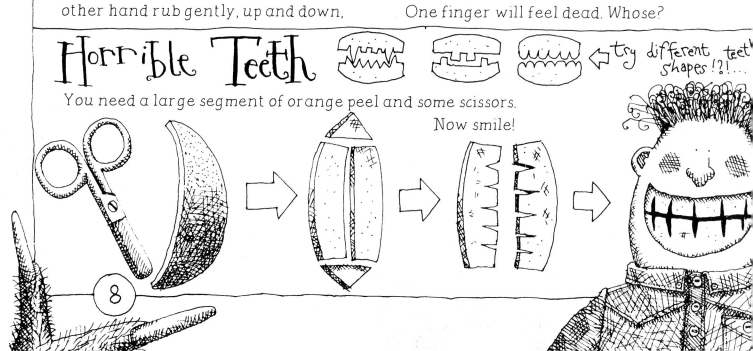

BiTS

one)!!

dience is feeling brave!

:ks are horrid!

Fractured Finger ! @ *

You need a pair of gloves and a small carrot.

1. Secretly, put the carrot inside the middle finger of the left glove.
2. Fold back your own middle finger against your palm, and then put on the glove.

The Missing Piece of Hand

You need a cardboard tube from inside a toilet roll.

1. Hold one end of the tube close to one of your eyes.

2. Put the palm of your other hand close to the far end of the tube.

3. With both eyes open, look through the tube and at your palm. It'll look as if a piece is missing from your hand!

3. Keep all the fingers of your gloved hand together so that the carrot-finger looks like a real finger. Now put on the other glove and show the backs of your gloved hands to your friends.
4. Hold the carrot-finger firmly by pressing on it with the thumb of the same hand.
5. With your right hand, grip the carrot-finger and then quickly break the carrot, yelling "Ouch!". Your friends will think you've bravely broken your finger!

9

Baffling Banana

You need a banana, a needle threaded with some cotton and a pair of scissors.

1. Push the needle in under the banana skin and bring it out further around the banana, making sure you leave some cotton hanging out of the first hole.

2. Now push the needle back through the last hole in the skin, and continue around the banana in the same way until the needle comes out through the first hole.

3. Pull both ends of the cotton and the banana will be sliced inside the skin.

4. In this way, make 3 or 4 slices. Don't forget to remove the cotton.

5. Now, offer the banana to a friend and watch what happens when it is peeled!

Play With Food. Play With It!

Take The Biscuit

You need 4 biscuits on a plate and 4 friends.

1. Ask your friends to take a biscuit each, but tell them that one biscuit MUST be left on the plate.

2. 3 of your friends will take a biscuit, but the 4th friend will not know what to do.

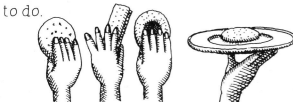

3. Show them what to do! Pick up the plate with the biscuit on it!

Solid Tea

You need a cup of hot black tea, some gelatine and some milk.

1. Put 3 teaspoons of gelatine into the cup of black tea and stir it well until the gelatine has all dissolved.
2. Let the mixture set for a few hours.
3. Now hand the tea to someone and pour in some milk.
The milk will float on top of the tea!

Sink-or-Swim?

You need an egg, a jug of water, salt, a spoon and 2 large glasses.

1. Fill one glass with water and stir in salt until no more salt will dissolve.
2. Half fill the other glass with water and gently lower the egg into it using the spoon.
3. The egg will sink.
4. Now say to your friends, "I can make this egg swim." Pour some of the salty water into the egg-glass until the egg begins to rise.
5. You can also make the egg sink by adding more water to the egg-glass. Eggstraordinary!

A Hole in Your Leg

Wear trousers for this trick.

1. Tell your audience that you have a hole in your left leg. They probably won't believe you!

2. Sit down and place the coin on your left leg just above the knee.

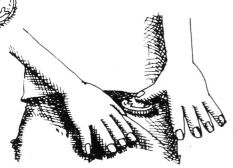

3. With both hands, lift up a piece of trouser material and fold it over the coin towards you.

4. As you do this, secretly slide the coin into your left hand.

5. Close your left hand and hold it under your left leg.

6. Hit the piece of folded material with your right hand and pretend to catch the coin with your left hand as it comes out of the hole in your leg.

7. Open your left hand and show the coin to your audience! Now they'll believe you!

Cunning
(Volume One)

Borrow a small from your audien

In the Palm of You

1. Hold out your hand towards your audience, palm up, and place the coin across fingers 2 and 3.

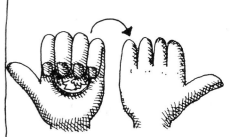

2. Turn your hand over, at the same time closing your fingers to hold the coin firmly in the middle of your palm.

Coins

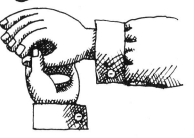

...dium-sized coin these tricks!

Now You See It ... Now You Don't!

1. Show the coin to your audience.

4. Secretly drop the coin into the palm of your hand.

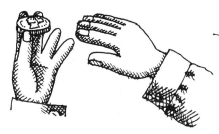

2. Hold the coin between the tips of the fingers and thumb of your left hand.

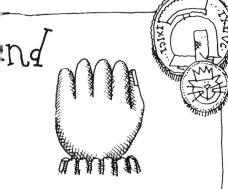

...nd

3. Hold up the back of your closed hand and show it to the audience.

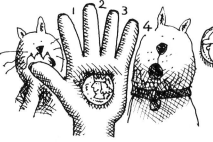

4. Now open your hand and spread your fingers wide, tilting the back of your hand slightly towards your audience. Keep the coin hidden in your palm and your audience will think the coin has vanished into thin air!

5. Take away the right hand, pretending that the coin is in it by making a fist.

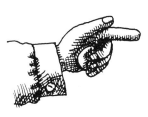

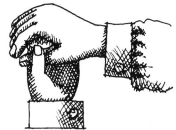

3. Cover the coin with your right hand.

6. Now open your right hand, pointing at it with your left hand - no coin!

Ear it is! The Great Coin Discovery

After you have made a coin vanish, here's how to find it again - in someone's ear! Keep the coin hidden in the palm of your closed hand. Hold your hand close to the ear and pretend to pull out the coin with your thumb and forefinger. Now open your hand and show your audience the coin. Think of other places to "find" a coin!

13

Jumping Rubber Band

You need a wide rubber band about 7 cm long.

1. Hold up your left hand, palm facing you, and put the rubber band over fingers 3 and 4.

2. Hook the rubber band with the forefinger of your other hand.

3. Stretch the rubber band and loop it over the thumb of your left hand.

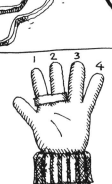

4. Bend your fingers and put them inside the rubber band.

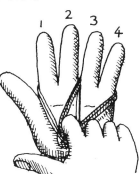

5. Now straighten your fingers, still inside the rubber band. The rubber band will jump onto fingers 1 and 2.

Colour Swap

You need two wide rubber bands about 7 cm long, a red one and a blue one.

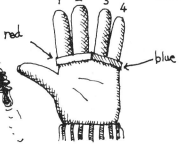

red   blue

1. Hold up your left hand, palm facing you. Put the red rubber band over fingers 1 and 2, and the blue rubber band over fingers 3 and 4.

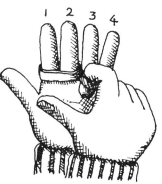

2. With the forefinger of your right hand hook the blue band.

3. Now hook this forefinger inside the red band too, and stretch both bands downwards.

ology

Rocket Pencil

ou need a short pencil nd a short, thick ubber band.

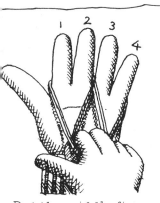

When no one is looking, ut the rubber band over our thumb.

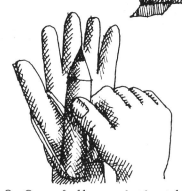

2. Carefully push the blunt end of the pencil down onto the rubber band, stretching the band down to the bottom of your hand.

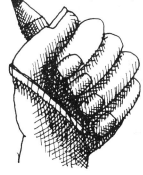

3. Close your hand around the pencil, making a fist.

4. Now show your friends the back of your fist.

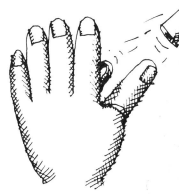

5. Quickly open your hand, and the pencil will take off like a rocket. Be very *careful* not to point the pencil at anyone.

. Put the middle finger of our right hand inside the wo stretched rubber bands nd open them out.

5. Bend your left-hand fingers and put them inside both rubber bands.

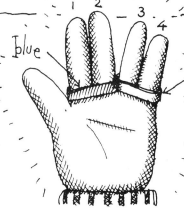

6. Quickly straighten your fingers, still inside the rubber bands. The rubber bands will change fingers!

How to Develop
(with a little bit of

Invisible Photo

You need a blank sheet of paper and an audience of 2 or more people.

1. Say to your audience, "I'm going to leave the room now and my assistant will make an invisible photo of one of you on this sheet of paper. When I come back into the room I will tell you who the photo is of."

2. You leave the room and your assistant holds the sheet of paper near someone's face for a few seconds.

3. You are then called back into the room and your assistant sits down with the audience.

4. Study the invisible photo carefully.

5. Now look at your assistant who will be sitting in exactly the same position as the person who has been "photographed". Then look at the audience.

6. When you know who the person is, say so!

To Psychic Powers
(p. from an assistant)

Bumpy Numbers

1. Say to your audience, "Think of a number between 1 and 10 and whisper it to my assistant. Then, by feeling the bumps on my assistant's head I will be able to tell you which number it is."

2. The number is whispered to your assistant.

3. Now place both your hands on your assistant's head and pretend to feel the bumps for a few seconds.

4. At the same time, place your thumbs on your assistant's jawbone near the ears. She will tell you the number by secretly squeezing her teeth together the right number of times.

5. Count the squeezes carefully and then tell the audience the number.

Pick a Book

You need 9 books for this trick.

1. Arrange the books on the floor in 3 rows of 3.

2. Say to your audience, "While I am out of the room, choose a book. Then I'll come back and tell you which one it is."

3. Leave the room while the book is being chosen, and then return.

4. Watch your assistant. He will point at a book which has NOT been chosen and say, "Is this the book?" You say no. But look very carefully at where his finger is pointing. Imagine the front of the book is divided into 3 rows of 3, just like the books. If he is pointing to the middle of the book, for example, it means they have chosen the middle book. And so on.

5. Now you know which is the right book. Your assistant will carry on pointing to books and you will know whether to say yes or no.

Ten-Ton Finger

1. Say to a friend, "Put your hand flat on the table and bend finger 2 right under the palm."

2. Now say, "BET YOU can't lift finger 3 without moving the other fingers and thumb." This seems to be impossible!

HOW TO DO IT:
Put your hand on the table with finger 2 bent under the palm and, with your other hand, lift finger 3!

Bet cha

Fool your friends wi

Gigantic Jump

Say, "BET YOU can't jump across the garden."
HOW TO DO IT: Walk across the garden and then jump!

Head-Poke

1. Ask a friend to hold up a hand and make a circle with the thumb and forefinger.

2. Now point to the circle and say, "BET YOU can't poke your head through that hole." Your friend will try very, very hard to do this!

HOW TO DO IT:
Make a circle with your thumb and forefinger and hold it against your head. Now, with your other hand, poke your head through the hole!

Words

se tricks with words!

Long Tongue

Say, "BET YOU can't stick out your tongue and touch the tip of your nose."

HOW TO DO IT:
1. Stick out your tongue.

2. Touch the tip of your nose with your finger.

Jumping House

You say, "I bet I can jump higher than a house."

Your friend says, "BET YOU can't."

You say, "Yes, I can. A house can't jump!"

Stomach Eggs!

Say, "BET YOU can't tell me how many eggs a person can eat on an empty stomach."

ANSWER: One. After one egg the stomach is no longer empty!

19

Twitchy Arms

You need a narrow doorway.

1. Stand in the doorway and place your hands flat against the sides. Make sure your arms are straight.
2. Press hard for 1 minute (count up to 60 slowly) against the sides of the doorway.
3. Now move away from the doorway and your arms will move upwards on their own!

Severed Thumb

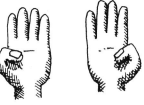

1. Bend both your thumbs.

2. Place your right thumb on top of your left thumb so that together they look like one left thumb.

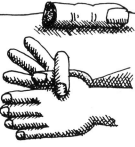

3. Put the forefinger and middle finger of your right hand over the join.

4. Slide the "top" of the thumb up the side of your left forefinger, so that it looks as though the thumb is being pulled off! (Make sure you show your audience the back of your left hand.)

Body

Test

1. Say to a friend,

> Let's see if two of my fingers are stronger than both your hands.

2. Place the tips of your 2 forefingers together, making a straight line with your hands and forearms.

Bits

(Part Two ☆!)

Strength

3. Now tell your friend to stand directly in front of you and try to separate them.

4. When your friend tries, push the tips of your forefingers together as hard as possible.

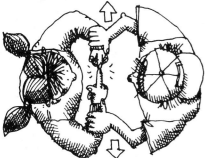

Your friend will find it very difficult to separate your 2 fingers!

Floating Sausage

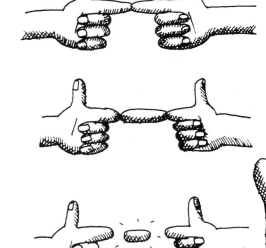

1. Put the tips of your forefingers together and hold them a little distance away from your eyes.

2. Look "through" the tips of the forefingers and you will see a finger-sausage floating between the tips.

3. If you move the fingers apart, the sausage will get smaller and then disappear. Turn your fingers to make a sausage with or without nails!

Finger Power

You need a chair with a back.

1. Look carefully at the picture.

2. Ask a friend to lie in the chair in this position, hands grasping the edges of the seat.

3. Stand next to your friend and press her forehead firmly with your forefinger - DON'T push.

4. Now ask her to stand up. She can't!

Whoosh, Clink or Splosh

You need a small, straight-sided mug, half filled with water and 2 medium-sized coins.

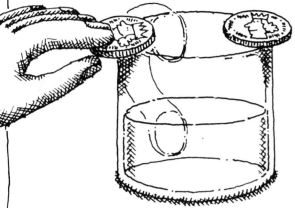

1. Balance the coins on the rim of the mug.

2. Now ask someone to try and pick up both coins at the same time, using the thumb and finger 2 of one hand only. Splosh! Now you try.

4. Very quickly, slide the coins along the side of the mug. Whoosh!

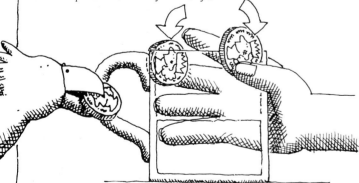

3. Using your thumb and finger 2, carefully move both coins off the rim and slide them down the side of the mug.

5. Snap together your thumb and finger 2 when the coins go off the side of the mug. Clink!

...ng ...s (Volume 2)

The Very Mean Giddy-Hand Trick

You need a coin, a pencil and a sheet of paper.

Tell a friend you are going to make her hand giddy and then see if she is able to roll a coin down her nose!

Put the coin on the sheet of paper and ask her to draw round it very fast 10 times.

Now ask her to roll the coin down her nose. She will be able to do this perfectly well. What she won't know is that she now has a pencil line right down the middle of her nose. How mean!

Two Heads Are Better

You need a small coin.

1. Tell your friends you have a special coin with 2 heads.

2. Place the coin on the left side of your right palm, head up.

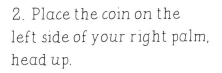

3. Hold out your left hand, palm up.

4. Move your right hand quickly towards your left hand and throw the coin onto the left palm, making sure the head is still up.

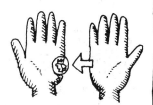

5. As the coin lands on your left palm, slap your right palm on top of it. Be very quick, so no one sees the coin properly.

6. Now take away your right hand and display your special 2-headed coin.

How to Climb Through a Postcard!

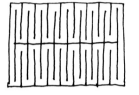

You need a postcard, a pencil, a ruler and scissors.

1. Secretly, draw lines like this on the back of the postcard.

2. Now show the front of the postcard to your friends and say, "I can climb through this postcard!"

3. Fold the postcard in half lengthways and make cuts along your lines.

4. Unfold the postcard and make a cut between A and B.

5. Now carefully open out the postcard to make a circle and climb through it head first!

Looping the Loop

You need a strip of paper 50 cm long and 4 cm wide, a ruler, a pencil, scissors and some sticky tape.

1. Use the ruler and pencil to draw a line down the middle of the strip of paper lengthways. Draw a dot at either end of the strip.

2. Now, holding the strip at both ends, twist it once from one end.

3. Overlap the ends so that one dot is above the other, and stick with a piece of sticky tape.

4. Cut all the way around the strip along the pencil line and see what happens.

5. Now cut all the way around the strip again.

6. Pull the 2 halves apart and see what you've made!

Paperweight

You need 2 identical pieces of paper and a pencil or pen.

1. Draw a mouse on one piece of paper and an elephant on the other.

2. Holding a picture in each hand, show them to your friends and say, "Which is the heavier, the mouse or the elephant?"

3. They will probably say, "The elephant." (If they say, "The mouse," ask why.) Tell them they are wrong!

4. Now drop the 2 pieces of paper at the same moment and they will land on the floor together because they are the same weight!

The Paper-Clip Link-Up

You need a strip of paper about 5 cm wide and 20 cm long and 2 paper-clips.

1. Fold one third of the paper backwards and join the 2 top edges of the paper with a paper-clip.

2. Fold the other end of the paper forwards and join the 2 top front edges with the other paper-clip.

3. Hold each end of the strip of paper and pull outwards quickly. The paper-clips will jump off the paper and link together.

Matchless Calculator

You need an empty matchbox and a pen.

1. Secretly take the tray out of the matchbox sleeve and turn it upside-down.

2. On the underneath of the tray, write the numbers 0 – 9 at one end and CORRECT at the other.

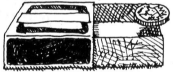

3. Put the tray back inside the sleeve. Now tell a friend that you have a special matchbox calculator!

4. Push the "number" end of the tray out of the sleeve, show it to a friend, and say something like, "Do this sum: 6 + 4 - 2 + 6 + 10 - 3. Now tell me the answer and I'll check it on my calculator."

5. Your friend will think very hard and then tell you the answer. Now push the other end of the tray out of the sleeve and show the word "CORRECT"! Wicked!

Collect loads of for the..

Money Box

You need an empty matchbox and a 1p coin.

1. Secretly open the matchbox and place the coin on the edge of the end of the tray.

2. Carefully push the tray back into the sleeve and slightly out at the other end so the coin is hidden.

3. Now say to your friends, "Watch this empty matchbox turn into a money box!"

4. Close the matchbox quickly.

5. Open the matchbox. Wow! A coin!

Mayhem

...pty matchboxes
...cks.

Matchbox Shock!

...ou need an empty matchbox
...nd a pair of scissors.

... Secretly take the tray
...ut of the matchbox and
...t a hole in the bottom
...ig enough to put your
...orefinger through.

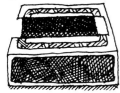

2. Cut a door shape
in the bottom
of the sleeve.

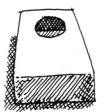

... Close the matchbox
...nd push your forefinger
...hrough the "door" in
...he sleeve and the hole
...n the bottom of the tray
...o that half your finger
...s lying inside it.

4. Now say to your friends,
"Look what I found in my
cereal this morning."
5. Open the matchbox and
give them an awful shock!

X-Ray Eyes

You need 4 empty matchboxes, a long-sleeved top,
a 1p coin and a wide rubber band.

1. Secretly put the coin in one
of the matchboxes. Put the
matchbox on your left forearm,
and hold it in position with a
rubber band. Then pull down
your sleeve to cover the matchbox.

2. Place 3 empty
matchboxes on a table.

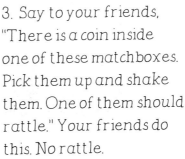

3. Say to your friends,
"There is a coin inside
one of these matchboxes.
Pick them up and shake
them. One of them should
rattle." Your friends do
this. No rattle.

4. Tell them you have
X-ray eyes and can see
inside the matchboxes.
Pick one up with your
left hand and shake it.
There is a rattle!

5. Move the matchboxes
around with your right
hand and ask your friends
to try again. Still no rattle!
Now pick up a matchbox
with your left hand and
rattle it. Xtraordinary!

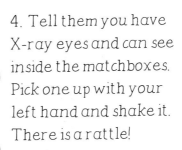

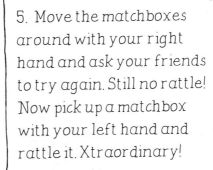

Thing on a String

You need a glass of water containing an ice-cube, a short piece of thread and some salt.

1. Keep the salt hidden. Say to a friend, "See if you can lift this ice-cube out of the water using the piece of thread. You must not touch the ice-cube with your hands." Your friend will try but will fail!

2. Now show him how! Make the thread into a loop.

3. Carefully put the loop across the top of the ice-cube.

4. Shake some salt over the loop and the ice-cube.

5. Wait for a few minutes and then slowly lift the thread – and the ice-cube too because it will now be frozen onto the thread!

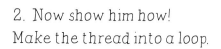

Climbing Comic

You need a comic, 2 paper-clips and 2 identical pieces of string about 70 cm long.

1. Roll up the comic to make a tube and hold it in position with a paper-clip.

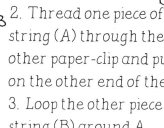

2. Thread one piece of string (A) through the other paper-clip and put it on the other end of the tube.

3. Loop the other piece of string (B) around A inside the tube.

4. Hold both ends of A and B and pull the tube down as far as possible without showing the loop of A.

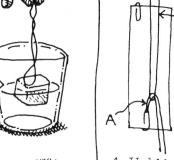

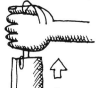

5. Keep the tube vertical. Hold B and gently pull on A. The comic will climb up the string!

Things

String Escape

You need a piece of thick string or rope about 1m long, a large handkerchief and an assistant.

1. Your assistant ties the handkerchief around your wrists (not too tightly).

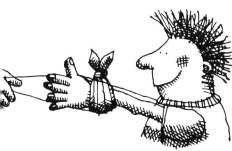

2. She then passes the string around the handkerchief and between your tied wrists and holds the 2 ends firmly.

3. Now begin your escape from the string. By rubbing the bottom of your palms together, work the part of the string between your wrists up towards the handkerchief.

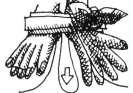

4. The string will begin to form a loop between your hands.

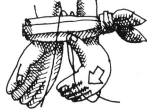

5. As soon as you can, slip one hand through the loop.

6. Now ask your assistant to pull the 2 ends of the string sharply. The string will come out between your wrists and you are free - but don't forget to ask her to untie the handkerchief!

Knotty Problem

You need a piece of string long enough to pick up when your arms are folded.

1. Stretch out the string on a table in front of you.

2. Cross your arms.

3. Take hold of each end of the string.

4. Slowly uncross your arms, keeping hold of the string.

Hey presto! A knot.

Box of Shocks

You need 2 very large cardboard boxes - big enough to hide in (one slightly bigger than the other), a chair, scissors, and music to hide any noise.

Note: this trick works best outside on a lawn or in a room with a carpet, as the boxes are less likely to move or slip.

1. Secretly, cut off the top and bottom of both boxes.

2. In the smaller box, cut a flap big enough for your assistant to crawl through. Get help with this as cutting thick cardboard is very difficult.

3. Fold both boxes flat and lean them against the chair. The smaller box, with the flap facing the chair, must be in front.

4. Your assistant hides behind the bigger folded box. You are now ready!

5. Ask your audience to come and sit on the floor facing the boxes.

6. Hold up the front of the smaller box to show your audience that it is flat and empty.

7. Fully open this box and place it on the floor in front of the larger box. Stand in front of the space between the 2 boxes in case your assistant can be seen!

8. Your assistant crawls quietly from behind the bigger box through the flap into the smaller box and hides.

Because they are so enormously impressive you'll need an assistant to help you!

9. Now hold up the bigger box and show the audience that it is also flat and empty.

10. Open up this box and place it over the smaller box. Turn both boxes around to show the 4 sides.

big

little

11. When you yell "JERONIMO!" your assistant jumps up and gives your audience the shock of their lives!

The Shirt Off His Back

You need a long-sleeved shirt and a jacket.

1. Secretly, your assistant puts on the shirt but only his head and wrists are actually inside it.

2. He then puts on the jacket and does it up. He is now ready for your audience.

3. Now, ask him to undo the shirt buttons at the neck and the cuff.

4. Stand behind him, holding the back of his shirt collar with both hands and count to 3. Then carefully pull the shirt upwards. It will come off without a rip or a tear!

31

...One Last Trick

The Crying Crayon

You need a crayon and a small piece of damp sponge.

Say, "Bet you can't squeeze your crayon so hard that you make it cry."

HOW TO DO IT:

1. Secretly, hold the crayon and the piece of sponge in one hand. The crayon should point downwards.

2. Now you are ready. Squeeze very hard. The water in the sponge will run down the crayon like tears.

First published in 1992 by Walker Books Ltd
87 Vauxhall Walk, London SE11 5HJ
This edition published 2007
2 4 6 8 10 9 7 5 3 1
©1992 Louise Cook
Illustrations ©1992 Alan Snow
The right of Alan Snow to be identified as author of this work has been asserted
by him in accordance with the Copyright, Designs and Patents Act 1988.
Printed in China
British Library Cataloguing in Publication Data: a catalogue record
for this book is available from the British Library
ISBN 978-1-4063-0635-4
www.walkerbooks.co.uk